BARE

(Truths. Anatomies. Absurdities.)

Payel Srila Banerjee

BookLeaf Publishing

India | USA | UK

Presentation by *BookLeaf Publishing*

Web: www.bookleafpub.com

E-mail: info@bookleafpub.com

ISBN: 9789360948214

First edition 2024

For the fierce fire at my altar.

*For your rock-solid belief in all things
prodigal and lost.*

For Ma, Baba, Di.

For my Son and my Son.

ACKNOWLEDGEMENT

To all those who have hurt and healed my heart, this book is dedicated to you. To all those also, who thought I was better broken. You have no idea how strong you have made me.

A big thank you to all things inspiring in the universe and that ineffable muse that is most certain to whisper in moments of utter nothingness, infusing my thoughts with all things brave. These verses would remain unspoken and unheard without you. To Ma and Baba, for making me the best version of fearless that I am. I am in hopeless love with you both. Thank you for being there, always. Especially in moments when I doubt myself cruelly.

Stay. Please. Always.

To the poets and writers whose words have been the undaunting ignition to my soul fire. Your wisdom and insight have shaped me more than you will ever know. Thank you for your hero hearts.

Thank you, people, in love and faith, who have chosen this book among so many others and who have decided to walk right through me. I am grateful and how.

Yes, indeed I have saved the best for the last. My Mumma and Popeye, for your unwavering, Gibraltarn faith. Jesus, how that scares me at times! You are everything I know of family and the most valiant and strongest people I have ever met. My worst critics and most zealous champions. These words are in print now because you believed. I love you. In this and all other lives. I am not allowed to thank them. So no thank you.

PSB

PREFACE

This book is a shameless obsession with the phenomenal in all things ordinary and hence stands heavily indebted to the woven fabric of life and its threads of love, hate, desire, shadows and the awkward emptinesses that dance between them. The words in this book are hence born of such inexplicable intensities of passion, unabashed courage, delicious darknesses and things often shied away from as blasphemy. This digging can be unnerving to the point of being scary.

What if you are caught off guard when you meet all that profound beauty inside of you, that you were convinced otherwise of?

What if you witness a stripping of the darkest desires that were your best-kept skeletons in the closet?

This book promises you nothing. Apart from you. In a space that is free and pure. A you, that is going to be in a way better place of accepting yourself for who you are. Sans regrets. Sans shame.

Say hi to lost love, its lonely whispers and its tumultuous storms. Know you are not alone. And yet remain unsettled with the searing intensity of all things hateful, burning bright against the kiln of your heart. Taste the sweet longing of desire, and the bitter sting of unfulfilled dreams as you find dark metaphors and ideas, casting shadows that linger long after the words have faded.

Bare your soul. No one's judging. It is so alright to be complicated and circumstantial. It is alright to identify with sorrow and yet laugh with sunshine.

These words in these pages were only my own. Until I let you in, into them. They perhaps may have nothing to do with you at all, at times, and yet when you least expect them to, maybe, just maybe, they will echo across your time and space, caressing things you hold most dear or things that hurt bad. There will be quiet moments alright, when you want to stand back and identify with the peace within, with the purge of your pent up through my words. And then there will be the blessed chaos and cacophony of passion.

Allow these a little bit of you, as they are almost all that I am. Accessing my inside was not easy for me. It won't be for you either. For sometimes there's nothing deeper and darker than the secret hideouts of your own heart. Maybe, we will just find the answers we have been looking for all this while, hidden in plain sight all along.

Perhaps, both of us will emerge on the other side of this book a little wiser, a little stronger, and a little more alive.

Table of Contents

Swallows

She wore the clouds that day
As the sun kissed her neck
Auburn
Under her prodigal mass of flaming hair
Like an ocean seething with forest fire
What had fueled her free was unfathomable
What had fanned the toasted wheat of her
cheeks was hard to tell too
The warm breeze which caught the slender
of her thighs
Under her skirt
Skimmed with stories of its own
Stories it would whisper to the golden corn
That nodded around her
Heavy. Pregnant. With fruit.
She was made of cloud and clear blue skies
Choicest of Cirruses.
Carved of Crystals. Priceless.
Profuse.
Lush and Luxuriant.

On a summer day such as this
On a summer day of tea and toast
You will see swallows in her
Find infinite of their own.

Prick

There is something stuck in my throat.
Something razor sharp and yet funnily
thick and blunt.
The sear is slicy and somewhat neat with a
coarse grinding.
There is a thick honey like dollop of
confusion stirred into the pain which I had
been feeling until now.
The confusion is hence sick sweet and thick
tenacious.
Dead.
Deadening.

It is both fascinating and familiar.
Like a family of unfamiliar strangers.
Seeped in surrogate strangeness.

The pierce is real.
The pierce is priceless.

Like a pulsating virgin vagina.

I have held on for too long.
Have let go of too much.
I have throated the dirge like a summer
song.

How To Be A Ghost And Not Know It.

It is difficult
I presume
Being a ghost

A whole lot of haunt
With cytoplasmic flaunt
And frill crochet and lace
With a very white face
All puke and disgrace
All epilogue sans preface

You would need to know how not to die
Even in death, in no coffins to lie
Or lie about being quite cold and dead
You should haunt, spook and scare instead

It is funny
I assume

How they think you have long gone
After the moon, into a sunless dawn
To a grave all grey they had carried you
You in white like a bride all new

Frustrating, I know it sure can get
When they wear all black to menus set
And wail and cry and scream and try
With unshed tears, and a lousy goodbye

Little surprise then, you stomp your feet
Creak up the stairs, pull off the bed sheet
From naive little silly kids, all too dumb
All too ready to fear succumb

You rock the chair and beat your chest
Oh do look at me I am distressed!!
They look at you and your hoary eyes
Your deadpan face and do realize

You are all shade, all ghost, all ghoul
But dearies that's a thought most foul
"I ain't as dead as dead can be"

You shout unheard, "You soon will see."

You are alive, why don't they see?
You think, you muse, and disagree
With ideas that you are no more
How easy they now, do you ignore

You are no ghost, you do regular things
Wear dandy dresses and your emerald rings
The red high heels make a proper ghost
Red wine, chicken and the garlic toast

You so still savour and hog in delight
You sit at their table under a fairy light
And waft through walls when you think it's
right
Spooking and shrieking in the middle of the
night

You grab ankles from under the bed
And creak doors open to fright and dread
The crooked crawl becomes you well
But you are no ghost, I sure can tell

You love cartoons and sitcoms too
You sneeze, and cough and go all blue
Dab at tears, and fall right off
Doubling in laughter or sneering in scoff

A ghost is when a ghost believes it is
Not knowing you're one is a cute li'l miss
You can't be a ghost until you think you are
Until headless or heartless is not bizarre

A ghost, one can be and not know a thing
With the spring in the step and a song to
sing
To know not what you are but live undead
Find a graveyard, red heels and a moon all
red

Do the foxtrot with the spirits galore,
Will you then be the ghost that all adore

Queen of cold

I am Ice.

I was snow last year
I was a little loose
On the beginnings of cold
On the hem of chill

The white had then become me in cuddles
In fistfulls of silly photographs.
On hideous honeymoons
In ridiculous snowmen and sunken boots
                              drunken pursuits
I had let you tread on me
                tread into me
With leather, you had ripped off from other
flesh
And wrapped around your feet

I had let you sink into me

Borne both your weight and back-strapped
burden
I had crunched under you
Made delicious sound of granular grate
To the chink of the beer bottle crate
Will you skate?
For a while among my pinecones
Of Love and Prick
But that is how I trick
You into soiling me sans remorse

You are senseless and nonsensical too
Your impenetrable thermals hide you well
One can easy tell
Well... almost most of you.
You champion choice derelict.

I scarce can contain my laugh
Imagining how you fret
For cottages of wood and forget
With crackling and spitting grills of meat
Atop mountains of alone hidden in me
Where your hideous screams of decay lose

For so you chose
To agonize agonies alone

I am Ice
Now
The edgy freeze up your
Vertebrae
I am more glassier
Classier if u will
I am transparent
And treacherous too
I let you see through me
Into parts that are certain nothings

I am a murderer
Of cold intent
I preserve what I kill
An undertaker of gentle
Of unsung abilities

I am cold

Unbrazen chill
That in itself is sacrificial
I allow you escaping moisture
As you speak
I allow you life
And the warmth that doesn't make you me

Where does your hate originate?

I have deeper, more vicious glaciers
My wrath is vicious
Dense
Epic
Look now how careless you have been
But I am fragile too
But you are guile
I am anomalous
I am anonymous
I am a bed
Of Caelumic geometries
And calculated glisten.

The Birds In Your Land

The birds in your land
Had a lot to tell me
They wanted to have a conversation
Drenched in distance

They sang of many a sea
Between you and me
Telling me to have heart
The one I had tucked into your backpack
At departures
With a kiss and half a tear

The birds in your land
Stirred the sugar lying
At the bottom of my teacup
Sweetening the sour of your away
I cupped more than the tea
I swirled more than hope

The birds in your land
Do not know who they are singing to nor do
they really care
They are in want of the knowledge
Of impatient visas
Of painful airplane schedules
Of allowances that allow less

The birds in your land
Borrow a little space of their own behind
your voice on my phone

They sing of happinesses that will be
Of hope that always was.

The birds in your land
Are made of sugar and sand,
Wispy and sweet
Made of the soft wind on golden wheat

They are songs of a punctuated space
That is yet to arrive at a full stop

Let them sing
More often then
Over the click of your stove
Over the tinkering of pots and pans
Over the sputtering of butter and garlic
Over the insanity of your cooker

Let them be exorbitant
Priceless in their freedom
For their song is a dream

Let them sing
For they have promises to keep
The birds in your land.

Taxidermy

I am in love
With the way
You start owning things I create
With your stubborn deliberate.

Like it was always yours in entirety
Since forever.

You make it yours
Like it had nothing ever to do with me at all.
My words become yours
In the thick of the night
In the calm of my sleep

You seize my words and possess them
You taxiderm them to perfection
In ink
You give them body
Wrench out the rot

And stuff excelsior
They are hence magnificent now.
They are hence infinite now.
Proud.
In a speck of things eternal.

The snatching away is a heart of a kind.

Your art in abduction is merciless.
My yielding, shameless.

Hard Boil

I am just suddenly jealous
That your poems will be for someone else

The words that you sun-kissed into my
blazing hair
In the prodigal October sun
Will flit around as yellow butterflies
Around someone else's kitchen window

As you hold her from the back and place
stale kisses at the nape of her neck
You get her hair in your mouth
It gets difficult for you to get it off your
tongue
On which perhaps my taste lingers still

The words you want to give her are the
cracked eggshells that she peels off
Cracked and crooked

With a hard boil

It's harder still to be so hard on yourself
As you sit in your fluffy bathrobe
Rare and ridiculous
With the early morning sun dazzling your
eyes
As it hits off the perfect squares of the floor
Flooring you with reminiscences of a long
gone song

A tune that unsettles you enough
                    teases you enough
By evading realization
It is here, on the tip of your tongue
In the churn of your belly
In the mindless throwing back of your head
But not nearly quite there
Not nearly a song enough

The song is long gone
The song was someone else's morning tea
In a cup that she held to her lips idly

As she stood smiling at her balcony
Cupping reassurance in the slosh of her
palms
Each morning
In something like a kiss.

How I Will Die

I will die on a sunny day.
When there will a lot of frolic in the waters
of my long-ago
The glisten will make soft music
And sing away silences
Both awkward and intended

I will have songs in my head
Lullabies of lore that
Mother would neatly braid into the glisten
of my jasmine hair

Then on a day like that
Of cockatoos and canaries and
mockingbirds
Wrapped in their songs lighter than
sunlight
It will all slip away.
The hate and the hurt

Most of the baggage
All of the burden
I will have no dents and no debts
Sticking ugly to my wedgy bones

The heart ever filled with love will find
water
The sponge of a lung will soak and suck and
bloat
In happiness

Nothing of what I will leave behind will
change.
I will though.
I will wear only shimmers and exuberance

The sun in the water will be gentle
cashmere
Warm. Wondrous.
Kissing birds, I will feed honey and dew in
cages of gold.

Condom

I want to be your condom
I want to be the lube
The dot of your precision
The ribs around your lungs
That slicks to the gneiss
Of your wicked desires
That sticks silicon on the love organ I own
I want to be between
The probe and the push
Squashed and smothered with jellies of joy
Untamed
I want to be inserted
Into your favourite privacies
Into the hole that you probe
In glory and muscle
It is me that will slurp your best intimate
Into the volcanic caves of the softest
fantasies
I will keep you selfishly

Within myself
Like a pocket of contain
Renounce the self to the masculine friction
Of your probe and mad groans
In me, your thickest veins will throb with
primitive life
Of ancient wants
Of unnamed demons
That will wreak havoc inside your choicest
soft
Bathed in holy juices of beautiful sin
I will hold your spasms of selfless release
The flood of all things male
The burst of the need that's primal
Barely real
I want to hang limp with all of your
thick liquid heat
Cling to you when even your passions have
drained you good
I will be there when you are cherished for
the man you have been.
Discard me then
Flip me lifeless

Toss me off into filth
Like I have never belonged to you
Like fragile snakeskin you have crawled out
of
To be new
Like I have never been part of your most
deepest desires.
Forget my taste
Forget my cling

As you lie.
In breathless seisms
I lie too.
In use.
In lies about the origin of desires
That drive you to be all things divine
And disastrous.

Rattlesnake

Welcome
To the wreck of me
To the pretty skeletons
That dance about in tins
Rattle dust bins

Bones bare that are picked
By bare fangs of starving dogs
Who hunger for marrow
In foresight narrow

You can find me
In the tear of your poetry
In the tear that she wipes
When you read it to her

Make me incense
Make me burn perfume

In nooks and corners of your favourite
privacies
Let me beguile you a little
With the blossom on my arms
Between the pale of my heaving breasts
Between my mounds of pearl
I will touch your glistening transparencies
Which you may shed at will
Like shattered glass
All too frail.
All too useless now.
In all your gorgeous slither and connive
But I know
You will sway to my rhythm
Curled in my bamboo bucket
Charmed for sure.

Little Things That Go

The day autumn drifted away
There was a lot of chill
In the air that hung midway over the city
In the crooked spines of people who were
more or less damned
Without faintest inklings

The day autumn drifted away
It carried with it most things warm
Like grandma's favourite cashmere draped
on the armchair
Like most of the rinds of oranges
And the skins of ripe alphonsos
It took savour and tang
Without flimsy innuendos

The day autumn drifted away
I hid my most favourite thing in a corner I
would forget

In a corner I did forget

The corner tucked away in forget

And for the life of me I could not remember

What it was that I had hidden

As I squinted up at the mustard of the

afternoon sun.

Umbilical Games

It is hideous, piteous alright
To catch you in your ebbing twilight
The day is done, so is the flight
The toil sweats into blurred eyesight

The unmistakable russet weeping into
The beginnings of a purple dark and true

I am rudely dismantled from ease
Knowing better versions that once would
please
A Hero. A Champion of my storm swept
swings
Of songs and strains and seagull wings

I spied you peeping diffident yesterday
Through tiny ambiguous slits of betray
Betrayal came smooth, it came silken too
With hobbling trust and faith askew.

But you are here now
As are they
You strive to tell
Grey from grey

And name the disgust
That lashes at you
Behind condoned silence
Behind differences that slowly grew

Behind the gentle nod
Behind masks all flawed

You still play dice in their umbilical games
You still call them by navel names
Names of love, names of known
Till they became names of being left alone.

Cigarette

The other day
I went up in smoke
I had stuck my butt onto your lips
To make you suck long and deep
In pleasure
And burn
I had raced through you
Mingling in your breath
I had raced on to the lungs

I had realised then that
A lung wasn't a heart.

And between the two,
I didn't want to inhabit burnt sponges of
loss
Or pores and patches of black despair
I wanted something much redder
Something more like... life

More alive
More vital
More prone to pain
More pulsating
Figuratively speaking.

I was about to end
Flickers of embers
Danced in me
Scalded with your kiss

You had finally let me in
I was about to flutter throughout
The insides of you
Looking for clues
To understand
Asinine cruelties
To uncover barbarity
Classic to you
Like smooth designer wear
Your favourite brand of imbedded vile
Flaunted finesse
Mall material

All glimmer and dazzle
I had envied

Once.

But now
I was inside the barren of you
Weaving in and out of your intended
Burn of breath

I lost Envy on the way out
Even forgot to hold her wrists
And help her back
Intentionally.

She cut a sorry figure. I figured.
There in the mire
There in the maze
Of your filthy sponge
She started looking more like Pity
Pathetic. Panicky.

Unlike me

I am smoke, remember
In the intermittent embers
You kiss to death
Yours
And
Mine.

Stuck Between You And You

There is a way how people born on a certain
day
Of the same elemental complexities
Are hopelessly attracted towards
repetitions of the disasters of previous
attractions
They rewind and play disaster on forever
loops
These same people fail to fill in their
presences with themselves
Brimming you with missing them
When they are stuck to you
Their absences likewise
Are filled with confused longing and desires

You can't then tell destruction, from
restoration or demolitions from creations.

The Butcher's Dinner

If there was ever a thing
Like
A favourite butcher
A butcher that carves flesh in practised art
A butcher who butchers to desiccate and
decimate
In slow poetry
In religious torment
In dry drain of the blood
Darling, my favourite would be you

I would choose you
Again and again
Over everything else

Bleating and braying in helpless ecstasy
As you wear your apron of murderous
intent
From my dark dungeon of definite death

I smell previous blood on you
Of coagulations around the thick skin of
your jagged fingernails
Which you pick at and flick off

I would look into your eyes
Where you have sharpened your knives
Honed your wonderous will to kill
You have done it before
And you will do it now
And tomorrow too
You will haul me out by the ear
Until something of the cartilage snaps
And you manage excruciating control
It is then that you will
Force my face into the butcher's block
With a thud hard enough to jar any residual
pain or sense
And let the knife sing into my skin.
Inch by inch
In sopranic dissever
In musical nonsensical slice

My blood from the chop of my veins
My marrow from the break of my bones
Spew and spurt against your teeth
In bare grin
You lick your lips
I sure am flavour of savour

You will sit around my escalope for dinner
With your family, forks and knives
As your greasy wife wodges out my veal
Dips it in sauce and shoves into
The full mouths of your overfed children
You will gulp me down with a sip of old
wine
Slam the glass down,
Fulfilled.
Dab at my gravy around your mouth
On very white kerchiefs
And tell her what an amazing cook she is.

Way Word

Poetry is inspiring.
You don't really doubt that with people who
know their ways with words
Or who
Know how to edge their way forward
When no one's looking
Gingerly on tiptoes
Between their words

But it is fearfully nostalgic.
Like a pain.
Like helplessness

Not everything that looks forward
Is progressive.

Headline

They splattered you all over the papers.
They spoke of your naughty abominations
That were despicable to say the least.

You were flawed
Now you are formidable too
You were wasted
Now you are woeful too

You plundered accounts and hearts alike
The papers murmured
The people gasped

You and your betrayal both
Wafted into early morning homes of the
deceived
Like the reassurance of fresh baked buns
You were here to stay
You were here to slay

Over the familiar curt crackle

Of the daily news

With nothing new

But you.

Flat Fables

We throw open our windows
To the soft summer breeze
That's cooling the putrid swelt
Of the day

Squares of our uninspired struggles
Squares of our nameless stories
Pop up against the romance
Of the evening sky
They pour out
Like thick coffee cream
They are alike
Unlike any other

The flat people
We have deceived ourselves long enough
Into believing our stories are our own

Into trusting our favourite flavours

Cooking in kitchens
Over the arrogance of pressure whistles
We share the same tales of indigestion
Acidity and politics

We share sweat, scare and defiance of
things viral
We wage wars on early morning commutes
Returning to our windows of space

I see you with your cigarette limp
Weaving your wear away
Cleaving your tear away
Thinking of things you can never have

There is a woman in a different square
Of a different surname, should you dare
There have never been words,
But nightdress and underwear

You wear less clothes and lesser pretences
Your window has no curtains too

You hide nothing, for there is nothing to
hide
The laughs you laughed. The tears you cried

Was her's as much as they were yours
The flat people of
Common fables. Common amours.

The Philanthropist

I touched betrayal
Loved its feet with my face
Cupped it in my breasts
Kept is safe
Inhaled its deep fragrances of a long night
Of stars and kissed wine
Purging all male that belonged to me
And yet was not mine

My philanthropist
Lay beautiful in bed
Naked. Narcoleptic.
Lay in my head.
Always with this prize benevolent heart
A soul that found peace in pieces

I knew of whispers
Which dripped of stench
Of much need abroad

A starvation that was infectious. Insatiable.
For new flesh and meat and hot saliva.
For intimate fluid.
I was to learn that charity begins at home

Hence, when it broke my fingers
And snapped my knuckles
With an ugly poke out of the skin
The pain jarred and straight kicked senses
out
The pain did not surprise.
But with the wake into the blur and stagger

The trust was abroad in largesse
The home. The hearth.
For all that it's worth.

Detergent

I wonder when you soak your clothes in
fragrant detergent
And they tumble across in a washing
machine
Gruntling about like a steampunk engine
from another time altogether,
Spewing out frothy bubbly water that is
luscious almost,
With the undertones of your aromatic musk
hormones
And swanky crisp freshness of detergent all
too sweet...

Do you remember me darling?

How much of me tucked away in the folds
of your bedsheet and your shirt from last
night do you wash away?
Mindless.

Do you trace my exodus from you into the
muck-filled drains?

Do you hear all my groans and ecstasies of
being a woman,
Your woman from last night,
Gurgling away in the gutters they cleaned
last summer?

I will thicken them and pollute them with
washing liquid froth.
Until all of me will become pungent and
putrid.
Until all of me is me no more.
Until the monster of the machine cleansing
your clothes and dancing like a Neanderthal
shaman,
Wobbling in possessed ecstasy,
Squeezes and wrenches the last of me out
of your threads and your stitches.

I am no more on you

I am hence no more anywhere
You are dry
You however are sparkling clean
You however are threadbare.

Soul Season

You were winter
Born of it
In it

Cold
Desolate
Distant

I met your soul half-way
For years
Over hot mugs of coffee
They make soft sour cream hearts in
The hearts you mess up
The hearts you stir up
For flavour
For soothe
For silk in the throat

I met you once

When the rain washed the streets of my city
Cooled the seething tar of new built roads
Settled the dust

I met your eyes once
Over the steam of my coffee
Over the wisps of memories
That I would soon gulp down
In fake reassurances
And close my eyes in sin and pleasure alike

I am the rain
Mindless
I arouse adventures
You thought didn't live in you
I found them
I fed them

Your half-way soul.
My bits. My whole.
Wiped off on the tissue
No big deal. Just not an issue.

The bills were now paid
Hurts erased. Stories said.

         85

And yet when I shot open my umbrella
To the incessant, relentless showers
To the thick rain,
To the fallen yellow flowers

I still could not see the other side of the
road.

The Keepsake

I wrote you a love letter
On the phone.
Over the crazy static of a jittery network
Which could not decide
Which language you should hear me in
But listen you did.
Just as I woke up
Just as I wrote.
And wove us into wisps of poetry
Much of which has been lost, my Darling
Words on Memory Tags
,s where I would have breathed and sighed
And dwindled just a moment,
;s of awkward starts and stops
...
Tell me you didn't know
You,
My Sans Serif
My winding loops of calligraphy

That

I have been etching you more often than

you have known. For you.

You have been reading yourself

All the time you thought you were reading

me. My pretty.

My pretty pretty heart

Less

Lesser

Will you know

How stifled I have been in expanses without

you.

How Amazonian in your mindless grasp...

You are the better poet of us both

I need words

Curdling and creaming at my throat

Frothing out

Into green gas feelings of war

You, however

Just need to look at my

Nubile, naked nape

And behold my love

I am the passion of secret words

And sly intent

The epidermis drips off letters

In the pink of the Passion Fruit

Drip

Drip

Drip

I hear myself plop on the floor

In pretty dreads.

...

This is what your love has made of me.

Childhood origami

Of colourful absurdity

Of awkward snip and stick

In scrapbook

I coagulate what I clean

I become what you make me

But I love becoming you the most

...

I am afraid.

I might turn you Dorian someday,

Mirror you to mathematical accuracy

And make you love me.

Our bodies double up on swanky hired hotel
beds. Body doubles.
Parallel parables
I have honed the habit of losing
Things of treasure
Bits of me
Of late I create in callous, clumsy
I lose words
Who loses words?
Things get lost all the time.
But Darling, you can go on.
Slay the day.
But
Leave me a map of get back
For my forget.
Write me.
In words, I don't remember any more.
Write me.
I am a keepsake.

Uninhibited

(I)
I wake up before you
Like every other day
To the peaceful rhythm of your stale breath
Wafts of my love moisture lingering still
Fathomably
Precariously
On tenterhooks
I imagine
in hidden corners of your mouth in corners,
That you will so very soon
 Religiously bristle and floss away when
You leave bed
And me behind.
I will dance and dally awkward at your
Adam's apple
With your gargle
Before you spit me down the slimy sink

Your mouth will then belong to you again
Entirely
As if it had never been in mine,
As if you have never tasted passion down
under me
Tucked away in tufts of the deepest fuzziest
black.

(II)
Beloved, I have always belonged
Where I should not have
Did "you" ever do the same?
In trust?
Your chest, my Berlin Wall
To which I died many deaths
In warm ironies of wrench
Beat my knuckles raw to insensitivity

I love parts of your body
You should know
Parts of familiar excitements
You become skin well

You indulge my taste

You tease with inconstancy

Your taste is exotic cuisine

Like

Till the back of your neck, and up behind

your ears, you try to taste of love.

(III)

It is the monsoon

Retreating

All cloud

All bloom

All gloom

When you wake up on me

Drool smothered, sebum smeared

Perhaps you will punctuate poetry better

I, on the other hand...

Feel happy on days of drizzle.

The smell of agitated city dust

Wears calm and wet

Tries hard to be oddly comforting.

The roads are darker, deeper, more sinister;
They remind me of your heart.

(IV)
Looking at you when you sleep
Looking at you when you sleep
Looking at you when you sleep
I see nothing.

(V)
I see the baby that you are.
Perfect. Young.
Hideous, wasteful, putrid
Inside.
I could have laughed until I cried. I could
have murdered you.
Remorseless
You are pulling me close
You are pulling me closer

Your blood is inveigling
The smell nauseates
It's getting me giddy
Stuffing my cranial cavities
Get out you bastard
Stop this precogitated impregnation
I am too vegetable to think

Can you afford a contraceptive pill? For my
art?
Pull me into you
Hold me to you
Give me a reason to hate.
Uninhibited.

Sandcastles

There is a munch of sand under the foot
And puny heroism at the edges of the
slumber and growl
 Of the Leviathan
Proud. Profound. Defiant.
The brine in the breeze
Bites skin
Making a joke of expensive sunscreen
The heavy hang of the cloud
Is purpose
Is the afternoon romance
Of a savage sun
The cloud has nothing of the wisps
Of nonsensical happy soap bubbles
Blown out of cheap containers
The clouds don't go away
They eat the sun in hiccups
They cling on to possible full moon nights
Tricking you into thinking one for the other

I play difficult at damp
I am in love with the flirt of the haze
In love with walking the twilight
Into nothing
In love with the storm in the tangled
tresses.

.....

Distance is cover here
It is filter blur
Across the haze and the sand
Bodies without clothes
Without faces of familiar
Shed both dignity
And wet clingy clothes
In obscene laugh

The faces do not have names
To feed gossip
You will never know them
They will catch the first bus out
Tomorrow
Before the wake of the sea

With photos of absurdities and silly for
show off
To last another year.

....

I decide
The sea, really, is not my thing
It is a lot like the inside of me
Way too relatable
Way too possibly disastrous

But the sea has sand to kiss
It has the fine sift of
Deep footholds
With every wave pulling back
You find bits of tiny fortitude stuck in you
Like delicious leftover
In defiance of its strength
It also hums forgotten tunes of chaos
As preludes to onslaughts of unsettling
calm.

Arabesque

I will act
For I do it well
I will pretend that you are still here. Act.
Because in an eerie indescribable manner
It's soothing
Embalming
Convincing even
I can pretend I am not alone
I can pretend I could look you in the eye
again
Share a squint
And familiar laughter
The kinds that turn you inside out
And split you up in comic
It is easy here in a spot
Light
If you will...
At this stage
You read

The chastise of ancient eyes
Peering out of primaeval skulls
Swathed in deep dark
Safe in anonymity
You do not have trouble
Identifying
The burn of doubt
In eyebrows that shoot up
In chins held in the arrogant tilt
Of censor
Of critique
Of the unsettle and inability
Of not being as good as you
And yet in outrageous audacity
Of knowing better
You would not have trouble
Sniffing out feign
You would not. If,
You were here.

I strike a pose
In my scarlet tutu

The sheer oomph of the outfit weighing me
down
I am a swan
Senile
Suspended between wobble and stance I am
moony-legged now
The third arabesque gets awkward
I am no ballerina.
I have never been delicate
Enough to hold on to awe
But I have often been alone
Alone has often been home.

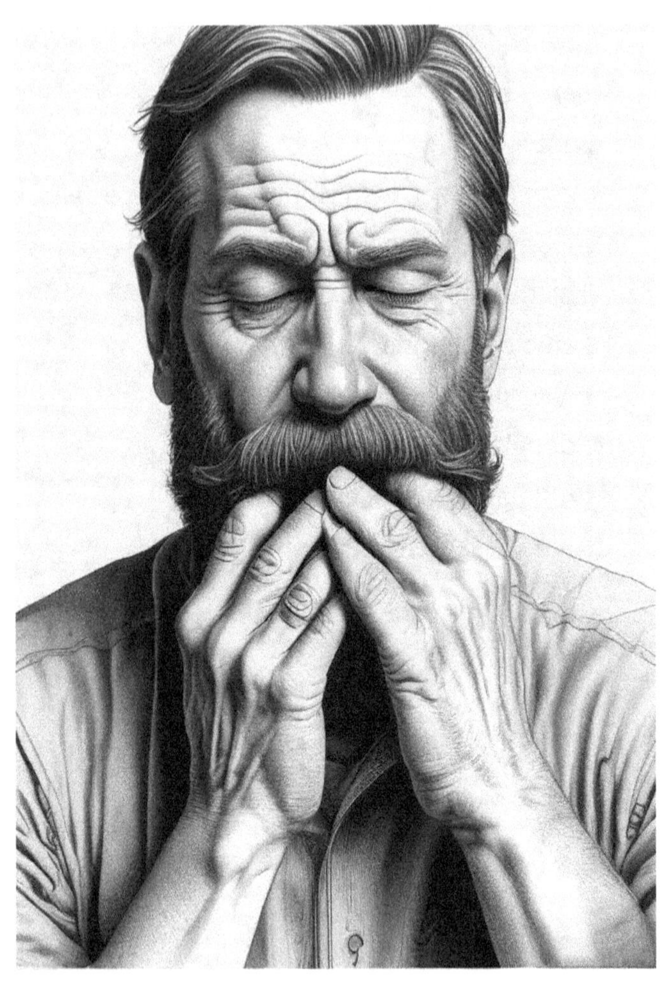

My Father Who Art In Pain

I have been around you for some time now.
Since you have been bending over my
freshly dug grave.
I see your knuckles all blue
From the cold
You are soon becoming
Stiff from
Clutching onto the fistful of confused earth
I see you slouch there
Without certain
Without decision
Like my favourite tousle
In your hair
All poke
All mayhem grey
I hear you swear by the Holy Book
On scorch kissed noons of lent
And by the silver jingle of Christmas pines
But I see you spent.

Bent.
I hear the split of your break.
You cannot return me to the dust from
Which I am
I flit in and out of you
Kiss you
Hold you
Howl in spasms
When you do too

The hurt is so much bigger than you
The pain in you is monstrous
The mourners are glycerine
You don't comprehend them
Yet. Father.
I have fluttered through them
It was easy
I didn't meet much
They are hollow.
Straw stuffed.
Behind the gross of saliva-threaded
mouths
The black lace and leather is pornographic

There is no mourn

There is no trust

The tear stains

Morbid. Vulgar.

I see them.

For what they are.

Tucking memories into my rich six feet

willow I can see the spite

Seeping through the jag of black teeth

They make haste.

In parting.

Giving away the little of me I would love

them to hold on to.

They pluck me

From their heads, from their hearts

They tuck me

Away in portions and parts

They sigh that I was.

But not you father

I have been of you

I feel you now

Like I have never before

It's easy now to inhabit you
To ease into you
I meet only love
Amazing grace
I own the shatter

Your hands are mine
Old and lined
Wired and brined

This is where you let go.
Now is when.
You do it.

Let the earth through your fingers
Let the lily bloom white
This is how you and I will love
I, the near departed
I love in passover
I love in vain
And you will love
Perfectly pretty in your pain.

Mothmap

Do not look at me like that
With songs of disaster
Which were always meant for forget.
 I remember the flicker
Of the thick white candles
That drooled with melt
I found them tasty
I didn't know much of destruction then,
With wings
Fit for the crumble of books
Brown and fragile with history
There were opium dreams
Of conquer
Of blood rage
My flit
At which you laughed
Was flight to me
And also
Many kinds of unchain

The pools of melt in the
Delicate nape of the candles
Were mirrors of
My flutter
Waxed in frantic
Before they hardened
Tonight was all that there was
Before the proud fatigue
Of tomorrow
So tonight I would
Sweat it out
In wing beat
In flap and futile
Before the peace
Of the tangled nettle of your hair

Nothing like a pretty butterfly
Before the wick can sputter
And blow itself out
There will be no charter
Of warm and good
No topography of prosper
Only fables of let go

The walls will not dance with my shadows
tomorrow
Nor will the unrest of the flame flicker in
her liquid irises.

How I Put You To Sleep

The distance does great guns

It gets you inside.

Assimilates

Makes fission

Before finishing itself off

So when you scour for your earphones

You clasp me and the night in

And set them back into your ears

Fumbling for reassurance

In your favourite lullabies

In the by-lanes of the unsettle of my sleep

In your cherish of my familiar funny

In cavities of ridiculous nasal gurgles

Reaching out

Behind the close of my eyes

Calling my name

In all the affordable soft

Of your grizzle

Awakening me to your unsettle

Ensuring my hold
Harder than ever
On a sleep that you need to cosy in on I
wake up to you
In kisses of unstoppable smother
Hurling headlong into you
All of you
Into a lot of your uncontain
Into your baby fluster
And it's throw-abouts
Into your fret of unreason
And all it's make-believe of exasperate
I hold on to you
And to dear life
Shushing the right alrights
Into the mess of your hair
Kissing territory
Into your head brimming with me.

Reptile

My lazy eyes
Heavy with professional drowsy,
Follow
Your reptilian crawl
Up the wall
In all things incorrigible
I almost fight the beginnings
Of the frothing bile of abhorrence
Threatening to ooze
Behind my throat
It takes effort to turn a blind eye to you
Or to the cadence of your stealth
I am all restless odium
I am also a toss and turn
An apex of pretty unease
As brittle as you
In tail tears and dead jump
All too ready to dump
Bits of me I cannot really do without

Bits that are my prize distraction In wiggle

In kill

In hunt

Hence

I will have to grow it back

For balance and stealth

Like you

In close scent of translucence

Under exoskeletons

In pursuit of the promise

Of food in my belly.

Lilac Kisses

We are of the concrete

Brick and mortar

Mortal

Prone to demolitions

We have iron rods

Shoved stiff into our spines

Unceremoniously

Up our rears

Of dilating disgusts

We have tried to scream

More often than your conveniences could

afford

We tried to tear

We tried tears

And are now left none

The pupils pain

With efforts at emotions

We have often tried to hum

The Lost Song of the Bards

We have often failed

The tune defies memory

A leftover

Of a morbid hide and seek

That least interests the seeker

It crouches in some old attic

In hiding

Forever

Nurturing the excitement of discovery

And peering through its rabbit hole

Unaware of terminal time-outs

Hence,

We have kept hiding

Like the songs we cannot sing

Or the goopy rheum in our eyes

When there's no tear

We are the concrete

We stand colossal

With little windows of stories

We light up in a quarantine twilight

We are many

And yet alone

We don't consider ourselves company

We have been pretty busy that way
To learn that.
Eventually, at least.
To consider the possibility
We comprehend babble now
And nod intellect
Until our mouths curled in
Deep crescent understanding
Make us look important
We are awful
And awesome
We have managed our own magic
As we stand in our square independence
Of our block of sky
Of countless shimmering galaxies
somewhere
You might not find us contained
In infections or politics
You might just find us far away
From our bodies you would call us
You cannot take away
Our building tops
From us

Our neglected oases of survival
It has been long now
We have started cementing our joints of
late
As if we weren't happy enough with the
hearts
Sure it is painful initially
They tell you
But we are brave
But we have history
Of easy adapt
We will accept the pain
We will anoint the joint
Malfunction
As one of our own
As a pain always meant to be
You are welcome
To our unlocked windows
Never mind the bars
They have recently stopped imprisoning
They let in pretty lilac
When day breaks
Which kisses our blushes

With hope
They cool many a heated cheek
Hot from a tropical summer night

We, the concrete
Have noticed little lilac flowers
In our cracks and crevices
Blossoming unsure
But happy
Wrapping fingers gently
Around the cool window bars
You might want to lean forward
And
Breathe deep
Inhale our souls
Which only return to us, the soulless,
In these hours
We still wear hope on us
Like our favourite perfume

One day
The lilac will stay forever
One day

They will not want to leave
One day
When you stop beneath our windows
To wave back to us
When we don't have to assume
Your smile
And call you in, to a hot pot of chamomile
tea
Like old times
Share silly tales of concern
You can then
Do your funny little waltz
To the songs
We now remember.
And kiss us lilac on the cheek
As you leave.

Destination

A speck of far
That lay
A little further than you
Was
A step
Made of many a mile
Of rocks
Of stones
Of waters hostile
The lines are dead they said
The comms are down
I smiled already, I so knew
Tucked away a bygones few
The wait would be long
But you knew that all along
Things are askew
Things are wrong
What with the dead words you ask
But didn't you already know?

Which greasy doubts
Which detach didn't grow?
My settle into words of ink
Borrowed from typeset
Of huddled soul mutinies
Of roses of regret
My page turner this
My masterpiece of read
Stories in the spaces
Of words I do not need.

The Return Gift

What have we done to each other? Nothing
much.
Really.
Just that I cut better now.
So is the edge.
There is a ton of pitiless razor-sharp.
A phenyl pit
Burning
Somewhere intestinal
Burning
What it should have cleansed
Disinfected
We are better mutated now
The DNA is loud and proud
With poems from Hiroshima and Nagasaki
And
A hell lot of lurch
And jump
And startle

And self defence mechanisms
There is also the mirror now
In epic idle
For lack of reflection and reference
I overhear it
At 3 a.ms
I overhear it's sinister hush hush
Of false wonderlands
Of misleading questions
Of misconstrued truths
Halfway between everything false
And equally beautiful
The butterflies are out
Of bell jars
And we frequent morgues more often
Lusting
The cold
And metal contain
I dare say we are now nowhere
Which is beautiful in
Many ways.
The oscillation
Is not chaos now

It is skin.
And everything under it
The blood
The arteries
The dung-beetle creep
I mean.
We are in little pools of precious
Inert.
Rare.
Gas.
We are everything to do with
Over eating
And acidity
And nausea
And belch
What have we done to each other you ask?
We have allowed each other laundry
The bedsheets are finally crisp
And starched.
And white and stainless.

Like steel.

Parrot Press

The machines are ever hungry
Maniacal in mechanical gluttony
They feed on the nutritious ripples
Of sheaves of pristine white
The incessant nom-noms are assuring
somehow
They programme copies hereafter
Forever after
On a maddening monodrone
The starts and stutters
Of a spit out in spite
Cursed in singular similarity
There is no break in norm
No prodigious defiance
No Promethean flare
There is however
Simple.
There is moreover
Rote reproduction

I am the factory
For that I have always been
You are the factory too
All squeaky clean
A factory of parrots
A factory for parrots
A factory of rivets and rumours new
Of brilliant green photocopies
Of constructed hate, spite and spew
We are satiating of the hunger within
A hunger that doesn't belong to us
A hunger that is now not our own
Our lost forgotten moral compass
Repeating that which has been before
And that which always will be
On blindfold, lab-rat bot command
We wear thick lies, have nowhere to flee.

Mascara

I am in hate
In a lot of hate
She announces
Unceremoniously
Bringing the shot glass down
Sharply on the bar
In a rap
Loud enough to get the attention she wants
Her eyes glassy
From her foolish grin and gin
She now has the desired scandal and vex
In the faces around
Sure
However
She heaves relief
They won't get past her heavy mascara
It has been more loyal than most men
It has stayed put
Through

Salt and sad water
It has slayed beyond
The flickering agony in tired irises
Beyond the wince you did not hear
Or the battle you missed
The heavier the mascara
The better the hide

They sure gulped down the scarlet of her
nails
With their Bollingers and loose lewd
They missed her clench at her glass
Her forget of herself
Is not for them to see
She tries hard to recall her face
The one in the mirror wasn't her
She was sure
She is sudden sober
In her newfound horror
Her palms get clammy
There is a break into sweat
She wipes it clumsy into the pleated polka
At her tender thighs

She cannot take her eyes off a nothing
She doesn't see on the floor
She does see
Hate however
Slinking behind old phobia
Hate has come clean
Hate has had honour
It has no lies.
No fragile false.
It will only overwhelm.
Like her heart

Hate is pious. Hate is pure.
There is no lechery, there is no lure.
Squeaky clean virgin hate.
Of puff pant moan groan
Of startle in her bed intimate
Her man in his naked stab
Shoving different flesh
Sans awkward. Sans shame.
In delicious defame.
His sickly white naked behind
Gagging a giggling groan

His deranged lubricated grind
Squeezing out a moan
The endeavour is a lesson in archaeology.
Primal. Exclusive of her.
She charters a course to the kitchen
Swirls hot cocoa
Plops on the couch
In unceremony
Tunes the telly
To a happier bandwidth
To a pitch higher and shriller
Of sink
Of calm
Of blur
Hums along her favourite jingle
Of nonsense and hogwash
Of exaggerated excitements

Hate holds her now
Safe and strong
Hate is all right
And nothing wrong
Hate is not little.

It is never a half.

How hate is sear and yet is bliss

Hate is venom in a lover's sweet kiss.

Honeysuckle

They will often tell you tales.
Tall tales.
As tall as they come.
Tales in which I wear red.
And chase the hurricane in scarlet.
Tales in which I am Blatant. Bold.
Bohemian tales that make a random
shameless whore of me.
They will drip words that they have long
brined
With the venom of their seething spite.
They will blur and blot my bravery.
They will baptize it bitchy.
Blasphemous even.
You then will know nothing of my sword
swing.
My war cry.
Of the fury of the wind in my hair.
You will be told to be aware.

Of my snare. Of my guile.

You will be taught to fear the thunder of my
heart.

They will whisper fables that I crouched
fearful.

Fables are fantastical.

I am Fearsome. I am Fantastic.

Legendary.

Look beneath my sheets of pleasure and
pain.

I am honey of the golden vein.

Of the thickest mustard sunshines.

Of Queens and Concubines.

I have bled beneath your shallow

Under your woe, your wail, your wallow.

You sucked me sweet.

For sweet I was.

You sucked me dry all because

Of the words you will weave

In intricacies soft.

 In slanderous deceive.

You will not tell them what a thief you are.

You will not tell of your murders bizarre.

Of Love and a Woman.

You will not tell tales of the murderous scar

Of Love in a Woman.

Tell them your tales.

Stories of a lying heart.

Stories with your treacherous art.

Hide. Lurk. Slink. Stink.

Bleed off in your favourite ink.

I will be Sweet and Shameless both

I will wear proud your priceless loathe.

How I married my son

{The tiniest truths and transcendental theories
of timelessnesses.}

One fine day I was heavy.
And full of life inside.
I was ripe and my flesh rippled
Supple.
Like thick batter and rich vanilla
There you were
Inside of me.
Flesh of flesh.
Meat of meat.
Soul of soul.
I had suddenly wound-up time
In all its magnificence and overpowering
awe and endlessness
With the umbilical cord.
I let you feed and nourish yourself with the
forever
Of a mother's blood.
You fed on me with no regret.

Why would you have any?

How now, why should you have had any?

You sucked away

And I bled into you

Every time making you.

Creating you.

You needed me to be who you are.

To become me inside of me

I let you feed on everything I had

For you chose my body and womb

Over others to belong to me.

I needed to keep you warm and safe.

And keep I did.

You cooed my name inside of me

Telling me tales of how love can be what it

was always meant to be.

You taught me religion.

Fulfilled legendary prophecies of time

And all that it had in mind for us.

The both of us.

You and me.

You in me.

In creating you.

I was Vesuvian.

Immense. Magnificent. Magnified.

So huge in the stomach and the

Head that the entirety of the

Universe became but one speck of

Sand in the infinity of time and its lapses.

You. My boy became the only truth.

You feed off me to become me.

And me you do become.

A split soul.

A body double.

Overflowing with overwhelming love.

As I screamed and flooded the floor

With blood and flesh and happiness

Of you spilling out of me,

I knew this was what God was about.

I held your toothless suck to my nipple.

Perked and plump.

Craving for the feed.

I could not fathom the direction of

fulfilment

I fell in love.

Hopelessly

Mindlessly.

I knew that old familiar feeling

That tickled everything woman about me.

Arousing carnal desires

I wanted you for me then. Only for me.

I knew then that I had to consume what I had created.

Flesh back to flesh.

As you sucked away

I smeared myself with your birth blood and plasma.

I splotched my face and skin with you and your belongingness.

I wed myself to you.

I sat there bloody. Married.

I sat there Mother.

Starfruit

I am in the wrong
I have committed an unforgivable mistake
Something I shouldn't have done alone
Something that can only be done with you
For you.
I dared a walk
Through the dingy of familiar by-lanes that
are promises of together
Been in a crowd that is more than people
Carrying our holy grail in our insulated
pocket of time
Suspended and singular in reality
In sanctae memoriae
Sometimes places are not just places
They are all heart
They are sacred ground you have
exchanged souls on
Of holy reverence and kisses of carefree
passion

Over and above

All the din and bustle and raucous,

Past the unnecessary of haggling old

women

In combat

With sellers selling the same greed

Just like the shop before this

And the shop before that

Past loud and cheap eateries

Dishing out delicious grease and adipose

With a dash of lime

And a sprinkle of time

Past the glistening romance of amber street

lights

With the sloshy, sweaty pork of the cook's

neck

Past shrill mothers,

Their musical red glass bangles and

hennaed hands

Feeding the son love and chopped star fruit

On the first iftar of Ramadan

A blessing and peace hence hovers in the

market at this hour

Your muezzin calls in my blood
A hunger and hurry that remind me of you
I need my son
My alone is hence an anomaly
Punishable
You are the branding of my heart
An unthinking, mindless owner of the
emboss
Of pure liquid pain and fire
Put your feet on my bare breast.
On my eyes.
In my mouth.
Make me eat your pain and hurt.
Make me tell you that you own me.
Never.
Never allow any memory of you
Without you
Never allow any alone where you cannot
Hold. Hurt. Heal.

Things I Would Be If I Were Orange

I wouldn't be blue ever
For beginners
That's for sure
I would be nothing near cold
I would not see icebergs
With Inuits or in Heads
Without melting them both a bit
Confusing and scaring both a little.

If I were orange
I would be the squinting tangerine on your
tongue
The sunshiny sour in your teeth
If I were Orange I would be the Supernova
of mindless heat
Sloshing in liquid fire

If I were to be orange someday

You could peel me off

From a lot of me

I would walk your spectrum hand in hand

From cold to things aflame

I would a phoenix be then

Sienna, crimson and most things red

Most things alive, most things awake

Most things zoetic, things yet not dead.

Sapphire

In my mind
My love for you sets you free
In my mind
I give you the blue of oceans
The sapphire of its waves
The sepia and gold it crashes on
At our feet
I give you the seagulls in free ecstasy
You look at me through amber innocence
And disbelief
I was all that you ever knew of the world
I was so adequate
I was so continuous
To you
You desired nothing beyond
Nothing bigger
Than the square of the dusk
On the rooftop

In my mind

You are happy

Free.

Enough

Not that we starved

Nor that we went without clothes

There were no smelly mouths

Or dirt wedged between fingernails

There were no maggots in dreadlocks

For want of shampoo

Or flaky disasters on diseased skin

There was no need to walk out of home

barefoot

Or thump cold car windows with

Fearful fake of hunger

Or angry abuse of want

Traffic lights didn't decide business or bank

accounts

But

There was never money enough

There was never money enough

To buy a car.

To buy freedom
For the five happy hearts
For the ring in the laugh
For the happiness of together
For the absence of the anxiety of getting
back home safe
For a maybe music on the radio
For wind flapping dog ears through the
window
And the warbly silly dog smile on fluttering
chaps
For the rearview mirror to be packed with
love
And carry home in a car
And having to leave nothing behind.

There was never money enough
To run away from pain
The kinds that excruciate
Kill on repeat
Or allow fancy holidays to lonely
mountains
To scream in careless ecstasies

On reverb

There was never money enough
To snub out the filthy stench of snob
That aunts wrapped themselves in
To buy father the luxury or the respect
Of the best seat in family festivities
And hence
The pain was allowed flow
Was allowed saturating soak
To the marrow.
There was never money enough to flaunt
Either taste or class
None to exhibit the art in the heart
Hence everything was written off
Highlighted in subtle humiliation
And the shy of a mother's beautiful
embarrassed smile
Behind the imitation of jewelry and
borrowed honour
Pride would hence chip off on flakes from
white-washed walls

Or hide underneath old and faded starched
bedsheets

There was money enough however
For undesired obligations
And for the weight of the best humility
For the cowering, under gratitude
For the intimidating threats to self-respect

There was money enough
To buy snide
To pay fares in piteously crowded
homebound buses
To never have to console hunger to bed.

Anno Domini

I have worked on it
Really hard
Trust me on this.
I have.
But your free radicals have however
damaged deep
I know because
My dermis is shrivelling in places
I can no longer manage to hide
Places
Where it's still less embarrassing though
I guess I could not wait in time
For age to catch on
Impatient as I am
Oh! But I am certain that you will excuse it?
I got my lotion off the local cheap store.
You see them all there...
The nun and the whore.

Betray

How now to the tongue would betrayal
taste?
How arsenic and full of waste?
How deep the stab, how vile the curse
Of sweat and kiss, and all things worse
Of slithers under hands held tight
Of daggers drawn in thick of the night
Of hope and love impaled, bone-dry
A shatter clothed in the prettiest lie
The fingers, they let go too soon
The hands ease into goodbye
Rats on a ship in sink, they say
Flee first, frightened to die
Betrayal is astringent all right
Sharp and edge in deserting flight
Rude and crude, in rip and sear
The conjure of your darkest fear
Betrayal is your make-believe
And how I, in destroy, hold on

How smooth you slip through in your
cunning
Until the all of you is gone.

Panties On A Clothesline

I let them waft

Carrying me to places I could not be

Into open windows

Of sultry lovemakes behind white

Bougainville

Invading privacies meant for two

And there lingered

Long enough to blush

To help romance the apparent mush

I let them waft

Into kitchens full

Of greasy steaks and unruly children.

Around thick mothers, the husbands want

to hew

Into lard stew

Mothers with pale clips in their hair

And chipped nail paint

Mothers in frocks of small printed flowers

Stuck in the unflattering gorges of the
waists
I let myself loiter in their blunt desires
Of what they once desired best
And now desire most
I let myself in
Uninvited. Unwelcome.
Floating around a shrivelling, balding
husband in sweat stamped vest
Hanging pretty lose at the growing grey on
his chest
His sigh sucks me in
In a flicker
For a flicker
I burn him young
I reinvent lost desire
Groping groins in jeopardy
He huddles lanky
To his blue window and gasps
Looking out to the white Bougainville
I waft Promethean in the poetry of
The ardent artist of the street
The penny poet of defeat

Never were they inspired so intense
Nor perversions purged free of pretence
You could no more demean, ignore
But stand applauding, praising galore
I clouded craving with a female scent
Brought content and happy torment
In satin and lace, sailor stripes and hearts
And perfumery of the most intimate parts
They breathed me deep as I wafted slow
They sketched, they rhymed with hearts
aglow.
I giggle mischievous around summer
flowers
And leave a part behind
Steal hues rare to find
And become them in parts.
I am now half feisty.
Half tranquility.
I waft under the light skirt
Of the girl they call Constance
As her bright orange curls
Dance close to her pretty freckles

My waft teases her undergarment
inappropriateness
I realize she has none on.
Her senses are easy to invade
I make her
Jangle the red bicycle on the sidewalk
In immodest haste into her lover's mouth
At the last cobbled corner in the south
The worn boots crunch the gravel beneath.
Her plump plum lip. His perfect teeth.
I linger a little in the spaces
In lovers' eyes, in their faces
He looks through me
When he wants to see
The girl he thinks he loves.

The afternoon sun is ruthless true
Glowering, prosaic, insipid too
It threatens to throttle and to squeeze
The pretty life out of my pretty summer
breeze
Before I go for yet another day
In this sultry, temperate month of May

I waft to the lilt of the heavy summer draft
To the turquoise of my Ionian craft
Tethered white boats ride the upthrust
Of the salt kissed shore, in holy lust.

Comrade In Awake

The monstrosity of concrete
Outside of my allowed square light
At 4 am
Swoons in a dark hangover
Of a yesterday that was
And is
Like acid burp in throat
A disgusting aftertaste
The gastronomique in you cannot much
appreciate
But there it is, nonetheless
Adding the sour on your face
And the tang in your teeth
And every other split hair feeling in
between

I figured out that concrete hangs on to dark
Almost
Sponging itself in

Like a warm baby bath in winter
I feel like feeling it's a woman
I see silhouetted
In her window of hope
Smoking
Going up in smoke
I am comforted
Across the ancient curious trees
Across the avenue

My comrade comforts me
Holds fort
I am her imagination now
I can flit through her head
Flirt with her heart
Heat her pretty groin
Wet her rancid mascara
I can comprehend the moisture
Behind the lipstick that cannot decide
loyalty yet
I locate indecisiveness in the limbs
That are long and long
For a body, close, quiet.

She wraps herself up in her own arms
Soaked in the alone
Of tropical night flowers
Heavy and thick
Like the drum behind my chest
Like the drum the lace won't contain
I want her to move around
I want her to be my soliloquy
I want to know more of her from this
distance
 Just this much and no more

Far will make it ache right
For these words to happen
Tomorrow again
She will have light
She will be up in resilience to the night
And I will never walk down the few blocks
In the morning with my collar
Turned up against the winter chill
She will be in faces at the park
She will run the mile with me
Shedding calories

Shedding inhibitions
She will be each lost mind behind smiling
morning faces
And be my storm against
The Bastille of the Night.

A Thing Of Beauty

She said I was to be a sketch
There was lilt in my sun messed hair
She said
The cascading softnesses
That flitted in fairy glow-worm warmth
Peeped out from behind ruthless showbiz
She said
Oh! how she would let
The graphite play truant with charcoal
And how there would be pretty poetries
Between the sandpaper and the canvas
Outside my window
The creeper crept in a pot
My city lazed out in a spring that was
altogether too heavy for my taste.
A spring that bounded into flavour
Too deliberate for my subtleties
I am a poet
Of crowded places

Of words that bubble out of thick noise

There is a certain quarantined comfort in

strangers

Eyes which don't flash familiarity

I am a poet

Of alone

She said I could be a painting too

Look into me

At the grumble of disappearing demons

At the rumble of terrorizing thunders

Look into me

At the weather-beaten circuses

At the trapezes over bottomless trenches

I am delusional

And now she would recreate me

Breathe life Prosperian

Take care

The invocation is shuddering pathos

Utter delirium

Comprehend the butchery

The bludgeoned coagulations of old

Let my sinews red

Flow black and white

In the few words fled

In your graphite that bled.

Things I Know About Loss

Outside, it is the vengeful rain
Yet again
Outside, the cosy of my cardiganed clench
Of the coffee mug
Outside, the steam of my breath
On the thick glass too cold
Making vapour of the heat of my hurt
I do not drink my coffee black
I refuse the compliment to my soul
I am generous with the gulping in
Of the unsettle outside
In warm cocoa tracheal quaffs
I stir the frothy, milky heart messy
In an entertain of confuse
I do not wish to identify the familiar soothe
I do not give the comfort a name
I bet
You standing across my street
In your blue raincoat

Trying a dry

Against a pour that will leave you very wet

With itchy underwear

Wouldn't notice

The knit of my eyebrows

Nor hear the clink of words

In the tin of my head

When I date my ignota sui.

On Loving You

I loved you
The day I found out
We could lie in bed, together
Undressed and naked
Unashamed of fake
And didn't care to do anything
I snuggled into empty
Miscalculated and did more
Into your bosom
Of strawberry sweat
And snuggled some more
I met your heart
Beating
In frequencies unknown
And I kissed it down
Six times twenty
Until you had enough
And pulled me close
Into your bosom.

Dart

I am missing you so bloody much.
Which means to say
Like my blood
That does dart
Straight for the heart
I want to touch my favourite version of me
On your mouth when you sleep.
I am so obscenely, shamelessly beautiful
On you
Lingering in your appetite between your
teeth
Looking at you
Touching the moisture behind your lips
It is difficult to tell you from me.
I pull you into me
Smell your sleep.
Kiss your faith.
Wishing I could hold you within
My self

Impregnate myself with you

Fuse you osmotic

I run my fingers through your perfume

Like the sunlit flirt of the curtains.

I need you.

Impossibly so.

Galactic

Tonight, I am going to make you for real
Tonight, I will blow millions of galaxies
into existence

Tonight, you will be particles of my
choicest dreams
That I do not stop seeing
Even on awake
Tonight, I will embrace God in me
Glow the Holy of Holies
I will flush blood into streams of my own

Pump it loud
Pump it pure
Till a heartbeat is there for sure
I will give flesh of my own
For flesh of my own
You will be constellar
You will be conceived

You will be woven

You will be weaved

With strings of hope

With threads of love

With all impossible power above.

Night Jasmine

I want to eat

Devour your breath

He whispered in unintelligible hoarse

I want to savour the tender

Ligaments of the air you breathe

Pick them out gently and

Let them

Melt away

Under the pink of my tongue

You burst at my taste buds

Tangerine

I have known ancient willow sap

Night jasmine

I have known

Flowers behind old moss

From fairy folklore

In the crevices of your body

You waft in and out of me

Like chaos magic

In liquid atomic spirit

He murmured

You are the taste of fire burning

You are the sounds of the crackle

And wood spit

The eastern sun in equinox

The wave kissed wet sand

He said

I will be

Magellanic horizons of your unend

Always finding a way back to you I will be

your triumph find

Your emblazon

He cried

Grasping cruel passion

Relentless in the destruction

Of hidden earth cores

He heaved in ancient volcanoes

And said

I will be your champion

Of Ouroboric gluttony.

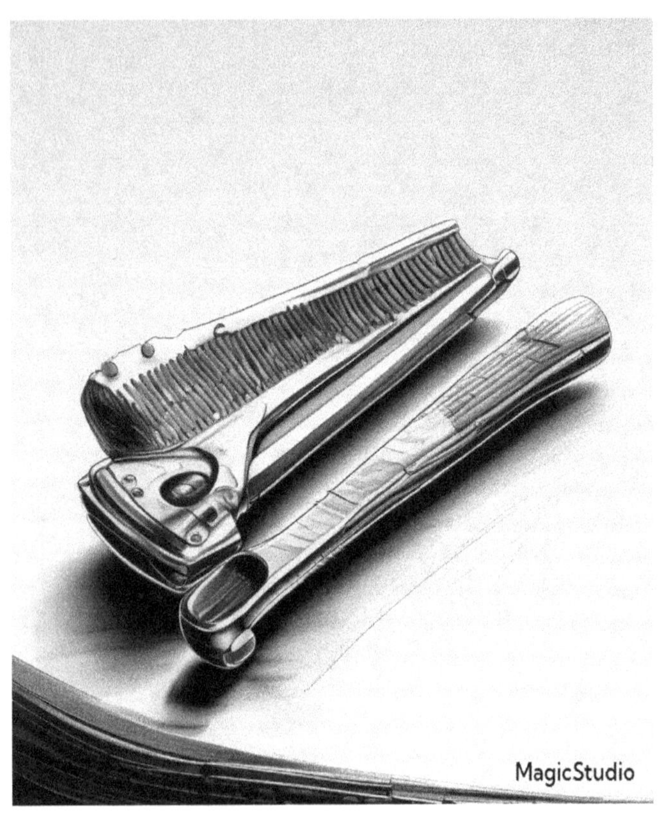

MagicStudio

Razor

There is something stuck in my throat.
Something razor-sharp
And yet funnily thick and blunt.
The sear is slicy and somewhat neat
With a coarse grinding.
There is a thick honey-like dollop too
Warm in wake
Soft in soothe
Knocking the senses out just right
In dumb thud
It hence confuses
In a confusion stirred pain
The confusion is hence
Sick sweet and thick tenacious.
Giddy.
All syrup.
It is also Dead.
It is also Deadening.
It is both fascinating and familiar.

Like a family of unfamiliar strangers.

Seeped in surrogate strangeness.

The pierce is real.

The pierce is priceless.

Like a pulsating virgin vagina.

I have held on for too long.

Have let go of too much.

I have throated the dirge like a summer song.

The Brainless Child

The brainless child had ideas wild
Was all chickpea and squash
Of trains and toys his head was full
Of muck and mire and slosh

A look at him and you could tell
How hopeless he could be
How fretful, forlorn, how weird and wild
How tempestuous like the sea

His rock and roll were loud and out
With the gramophone on loop
With throws and jumps and flips and flops
With staggering stance and swoop

The brainless child set sail one night
In a boat all stuffed with awe
In search of The Land of The Blazing Sun
For fire and ancient lore
The rockstar, was a warrior too

The kinds that are rare today
Extinct even to a fault
The breed that would never betray

So 'gainst the wind, he unfurled his sails
Kissed his soil goodbye
Strummed his guitar, threw hair 'bout
Whimpered a war cry

No army did this brave heart lead
No fleet of ships to sail
With a heart, the core of a flaming torch
He braved the snow and hail

Monsters, ogres, gargoyles all
He was sure to slay and bind
A better epic or glorious legend
Would indeed be hard to find

So Brainless being all bone and skin
And a bowl for a helmet donning
Set sail into the rising moon
With kids on shore all fawning

What battles he won, which wars he fought
No one can surely tell
Which victories won, or monsters caught
On whom he wrecked much hell

His story is no fireside lore
For a cause does a hero make
No cause here and no hero hence
For all the Good Lord's sake.

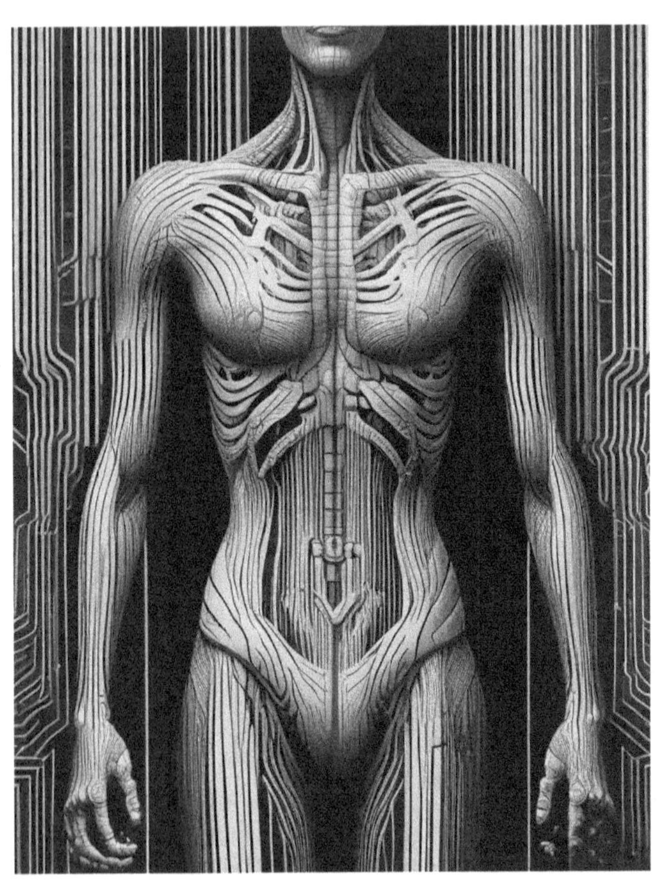

Lie

Lies

Lie flat

Lie flagrant

In fragrance that slink around lies

As I lie

Flat

Linear

Line lies

Thin lines

Between open worlds

Split

Parallel

Of truths from a probable

Probable parallels

Parallel lines

Analogous lies

Different dots

Of start. Of stop

Together

Geometric

Correct. Cardinal.

Of probable lies

From different worlds

Parallel lies

Nowhere truths

Your favourite gospel axioms.

Radio Heart

My heart is a radio
Atop your shelf
Of dust and lust
Both forgotten
There are red oleanders growing
Out of me
With leaves
Which leaves
Me useless. Beautiful.
Some bird unknown
Dropped a seed
Into my wide gaping mouth
You forgot to shut
After you scraped out the entangled tape
Snapped it somewhere mid-song
I stuttered and spitted
At your wrench at my knobs
I blossomed and bloomed
At your shelving of me

Don't think to think of me

In misleading mellifluous melodies

Under your breath

On non-existent keys

Sing songing of distant truancies

Lurking in lunacies

Walking on sunny fields caressing

dandelions

Which kiss the lace at the hem of your skirt

The tape is a shimmering snare

Catching the dusty setting sun

On the creaky cabin floor

Wedged ugly

Between the boards

I am a radio

Of forlorn

And forget

That no curious child

With dirty fingernails

Can dismantle or beat or batter

Just enough

To get me cough up old rust

I am here

Here I will be

Stuck in the mires of unforgiving memory

Stuck between the need to make music

And the need to bloom red.

Iscariot

You lie in beauty
They say you wrap them well
In unforgivable forevers
In a shroud you stole
From the End of Times.
You whisper in poison
Your hiss is made of burn
A mathematical precision
Of intend
Of intense
And lechery
How now you do it flawless?
Perfection, they say, comes at a price.
What has been your pay?
The writhe in the gut
The slit in the soul
The carbuncle of greed in green
You are elegant
In spite

You are Botox

On your pout

The flesh is engineered

For no feel

I am no fool

I know how a kiss can betray

Better in silicone

And swell

So when you plant one

On the fume of my cheek

In effortless conniving

And easy conspiracies

Of fatal things

I hear the clink of your silver

Of sold

Hang loose around your groin

And know how heavy my cross will be

You are a breakthrough in broken

You champion slither around apples all red

You are my robin redbreast

The Iscariot of my Sacred Heart.